D0721135

Just Joking

ARCTURUS

This edition published in 2017 by Arcturus Publishing Limited
26/27 Bickels Yard, 151–153 Bermondsey Street,
London SE1 3HA

ISBN: 978-1-78428-479-4
CH005153NT
Supplier 29, Date 0517, Print run 5779

Written by Lisa Regan
Illustrated by Shutterstock
Designed by Trudi Webb
Edited by Tracey Kelly

Printed in China

CONTENTS

CONTENTS

TERRIBLE TRAVEL

HOW DO LIGHTHOUSE KEEPERS COMMUNICATE WITH EACH OTHER?

WITH SHINE LANGUAGE!

WHAT CAN FLY UNDERWATER?

A WASP IN A SUBMARINE!

WHAT DO YOU USE TO CUT THE OCEAN IN TWO?

A SEASAW!

WHAT IS BIG, FURRY, AND FLIES?

A HOT-AIR BABOON!

6

WHAT DO THEY SING ON YOUR BIRTHDAY IN ICELAND?

"FREEZE A JOLLY GOOD FELLOW!"

WHEN IS A BOAT LIKE A PILE OF SNOW?

WHEN IT'S ADRIFT!

WHAT FALLS AT THE NORTH POLE BUT NEVER GETS HURT?

SNOW!

WHAT DO YOU CALL A STRANDED POLAR BEAR?

ICE-OLATED!

WHAT'S THE SMALLEST STATE IN THE US?

MINI-SOTA!

WHERE DO PIANISTS GO FOR SOME SUNSHINE?

THE FLORIDA KEYS!

WHAT DID TENNESSEE?

THE SAME THING ARKAN-SAW!

WHICH STATE SNEEZES THE MOST?

MASS-ACHOO-SETTS!

9

WHAT DO YOU CALL A HAPPY ONE-LEGGED PIRATE?

A HOP-TIMIST!

WHY WAS THE PIRATE FEELING SAD?

LONG TIME, NO SEA.

WHAT MUSIC DO PIRATES LISTEN TO?

SOLE MUSIC!

HOW MUCH DO PIRATES PAY TO GET THEIR EARS PIERCED?

A BUCK AN EAR!

WHAT HAPPENS WHEN A PIRATE SHIP GETS OLD?

IT KEELS OVER!

WHY DID THE PIRATE GIVE HIS SHIP A COAT OF PAINT?

BECAUSE ITS TIMBERS WERE SHIVERING!

WHY DID THE PIRATE LEAVE A CHICKEN WITH HIS BURIED TREASURE?

BECAUSE EGGS MARKS THE SPOT!

HOW DO YOU ANNOY A PIRATE?

TAKE AWAY THE P TO MAKE HIM IRATE!

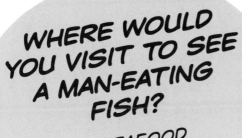

WHERE WOULD YOU VISIT TO SEE A MAN-EATING FISH?

A SEAFOOD RESTAURANT!

WHY DID THE SAILOR CROSS THE ROAD?

TO GET TO THE OTHER TIDE!

HOW DID THE CAPTAIN DO AT SCHOOL?

HE GOT HIGH Cs!

WHAT SORT OF FOOD CAN YOU BUY ON A CHINESE BOAT?

JUNK FOOD!

WHY DON'T ASTRONAUTS GET ALONG WELL WITH MANY PEOPLE?

THEY'RE NOT REALLY DOWN TO EARTH.

HOW DOES AN ASTRONAUT GET HIS BABY TO SLEEP?

ROCKET!

WHY COULDN'T THE ASTRONAUT LAND ON THE MOON?

BECAUSE IT WAS FULL!

WHAT DOES AN ASTRONAUT HAVE IN THE BACK OF THE CAR?

A BOOSTER SEAT!

WHY DO ASTRONAUTS TAKE SANDWICHES ON BOARD THEIR ROCKET?

THEY GET HUNGRY AT LAUNCH TIME!

WHY DON'T ASTRONAUTS HAVE LONG CAREERS?

BECAUSE AFTER THEIR TRAINING, THEY GET FIRED!

WHAT DO ASTRONAUTS DRINK WITH THEIR CAKE?

GRAVI-TEA!

WHAT DOES AN ASTRONAUT DO WHEN HIS TOENAILS ARE TOO LONG?

ECLIPSE THEM!

WHAT DO YOU SAY TO A FROG THAT IS HITCHING A RIDE?

"HOP IN!"

HAVE YOU FINISHED READING THE STORY OF THE MOTOR CAR?

NO, I'VE DECIDED I DON'T LIKE AUTOBIOGRAPHIES!

WHAT'S THE BEST CAR FOR DRIVING THROUGH WATER?

A FORD!

DID YOU HEAR ABOUT THE FROG THAT PARKED ILLEGALLY?

IT GOT TOAD AWAY!

WHAT DO YOU CALL A PIRATE WITH WOODEN ARMS AND LEGS?

BOB!

WHY DID THE PIRATE VISIT THE COMPUTER STORE?

TO BUY AN IPATCH!

WHAT PIZZA TOPPING DO PIRATES LIKE BEST?

ARRRRRRTICHOKES!

HOW DO YOU GET RID OF A ONE-LEGGED PIRATE?

TELL HIM TO HOP IT!

WHEN'S THE BEST TIME TO BUY A PIRATE SHIP?

WHEN THEY'RE ON SAIL!

HOW DOES A PIRATE TRAVEL WHEN HE'S ON LAND?

BY CARRRRRRR!

WHY CAN'T YOU TAKE A PHOTO OF A PIRATE WITH A WOODEN LEG?

BECAUSE WOODEN LEGS DON'T TAKE PHOTOS!

WHAT DID THE PIRATE SAY WHEN HE TRAPPED HIS WOODEN LEG IN THE FREEZER?

"SHIVER ME TIMBERS!"

WHAT'S THE BEST WAY TO CROSS THE OCEAN?

BY TAXI-CRAB!

WHAT KEEPS ON RUNNING WITHOUT GETTING TIRED?

A RIVER!

WHAT DO YOU GET IF YOU MEET A SHARK IN THE ARCTIC OCEAN?

FROSTBITE!

WHY WOULD YOU TAKE A BASEBALL GLOVE ON A SURFING TRIP?

SO YOU CAN CATCH A WAVE!

WHAT DID THE CRUISE LINER SAY AS IT SAILED INTO PORT?

"WHAT'S UP, DOCK?"

DID YOU HEAR ABOUT THE CUDDLY SEA CAPTAIN?

HE LIKED TO HUG THE SHORE!

WHAT DO YOU NEED TO DRIVE YOUR CAR ALONG THE BEACH?

FOUR-EEL DRIVE!

HOW DO YOU GET TO SEE A SCHOOL OF FISH?

TRAVEL BY OCTOBUS!

WHERE DO PENGUINS GO TO VOTE?

THE SOUTH POLL!

WHAT'S THE BEST THING TO DO ON A TRIP TO THE ARCTIC?

JUST CHILL.

CAN YOU NAME FIVE ANIMALS FOUND AT THE NORTH POLE?

"FOUR SEALS AND A POLAR BEAR?"

WHY DID THE POLAR BEAR CROSS THE ROAD?

TO GO WITH THE FLOE!

WHY SHOULD YOU NEVER ARGUE ON A HOT-AIR BALLOON RIDE?

YOU DON'T WANT TO FALL OUT!

WHERE IS HADRIAN'S WALL?

AROUND HADRIAN'S GARDEN!

WHICH ANIMAL WAS THE FIRST IN SPACE?

THE COW WHO JUMPED OVER THE MOON!

WHAT KIND OF HOUSE WEIGHS THE LEAST?

A LIGHTHOUSE!

WHAT DO YOU CALL A TOY TRAIN SET?

A PLAY STATION!

WHY DON'T ELEPHANTS TRAVEL BY TRAIN?

THEY DON'T LIKE PUTTING THEIR TRUNKS ON THE LUGGAGE RACK!

WHY DID THE TRAIN DRIVER GET FIRED?

HE WAS TOO EASILY SIDE-TRACKED!

WHERE CAN YOU BUY A TRAIN TERMINUS?

AN END-OF-LINE SALE!

WHY DID THE
BRIDGE GET
ANGRY?
BECAUSE PEOPLE WERE
ALWAYS CROSSING IT!

WHEN IS A
CAR NOT
A CAR?

WHEN IT
TURNS INTO
A DRIVEWAY.

WHAT DO YOU
GET IF YOU
RUN BEHIND A
CAR?

EXHAUSTED!

WHY DID THE
LITTLE CAR STOP
WHEN IT SAW THE
MONSTER TRUCK?

IT HAD A NERVOUS
BREAKDOWN!

WHAT IS THE HARDEST THING WHEN YOU LEARN TO RIDE A BIKE?

THE GROUND!

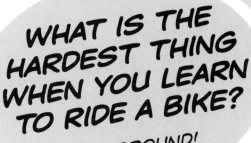

WHAT DID THE BABY BICYCLE CALL ITS FATHER?

POP-CYCLE!

HOW DID THE HAIRDRESSER WIN THE CYCLE RACE?

SHE TOOK A SHORTCUT!

HOW DID THE CYCLIST GET A PUNCTURE?

SHE DIDN'T SEE THE FORK IN THE ROAD!

WHAT DO YOU CALL A LAZY BABY KANGAROO?

A POUCH POTATO!

WHAT DO YOU CALL A BOOMERANG THAT DOESN'T COME BACK?

A STICK!

WHY DO KANGAROOS HATE BAD WEATHER?

BECAUSE THE KIDS HAVE TO PLAY INDOORS!

WHAT ANIMAL CAN JUMP HIGHER THAN SYDNEY OPERA HOUSE?

ALL ANIMALS, BECAUSE THE OPERA HOUSE CAN'T JUMP!

WHAT'S IN THE MIDDLE OF AUSTRALIA?

THE LETTER R!

WHY DID THE EMU CROSS THE ROAD?

TO PROVE IT WASN'T CHICKEN!

WHAT DO YOU GET IF YOU CROSS A KANGAROO AND AN ELEPHANT?

GREAT BIG HOLES ALL OVER AUSTRALIA!

WHAT'S SMALL, FURRY, AND PURPLE?

A KOALA HOLDING ITS BREATH!

WHAT BIRD IS COMMONLY FOUND IN PORTUGAL?

PORTU-GEESE!

WHAT DO INUIT PEOPLE USE TO HOLD THEIR HOUSES TOGETHER?

IGLUE!

WHAT DO YOU CALL A SPANIARD WHO CAN'T FIND HIS CAR?

CARLOS!

WHICH IS THE MOST POLITE TOURIST ATTRACTION IN THE WORLD?

THE LEANING TOWER OF PLEASE-A!

WHY DO THE FRENCH LOVE TO EAT SNAILS?

THEY DON'T LIKE FAST FOOD!

WHAT'S PURPLE AND FISHY AND FOUND OFF THE COAST OF AUSTRALIA?

THE GRAPE BARRIER REEF!

WHICH CAPITAL CITY IS GROWING AT THE FASTEST RATE?

DUBLIN!

DID YOU HEAR ABOUT THE MAN WHO JUMPED OFF A BRIDGE IN PARIS?

HE WAS IN SEINE!

39

WHAT GAME DO ASTRONAUTS PLAY TO KILL THE TIME?

MOON-OPOLY!

WHAT DO ASTRONAUTS WEAR WHEN THEY AREN'T IN THEIR SPACE SUITS?

APOLLO SHIRTS!

WHAT KIND OF MUSIC DO ASTRONAUTS LIKE?

ROCKET AND ROLL!

WHAT INJECTIONS DOES AN ASTRONAUT HAVE BEFORE A TRIP?

BOOSTER SHOTS!

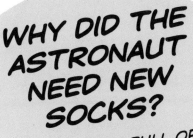

WHY DID THE ASTRONAUT NEED NEW SOCKS?

HERS WERE FULL OF BLACK HOLES!

WHAT GOES MOOZ?

A SPACESHIP REVERSING!

WHY DID THE ASTRONAUTS MOVE TO A NEW HOUSE?

THEY WERE SPACED OUT!

HOW MANY PLANETS ARE OUT IN SPACE?

ALL OF THEM!

WHICH RIVER DO SNAKE HUNTERS FLOCK TO?

THE HISSISSIPPI!

WHAT DO YOU CALL A COUNTRY WHERE EVERYONE DRIVES A PINK CAR?

A PINK CAR-NATION!

WHAT WAS THE HIGHEST MOUNTAIN BEFORE EVEREST WAS DISCOVERED?

STILL MOUNT EVEREST!

WHERE CAN YOU FIND THE ANDES?

AT THE END OF YOUR ARMIES!

WHAT HAPPENED TO THE FAIRY WHO SKIPPED SCHOOL?

SHE WAS EX-SPELLED!

WHAT DO FAIRIES USE TO TIE BACK THEIR HAIR?

RAINBOWS!

WHAT DO YOU CALL A FAIRY THAT NEVER TAKES A BATH?

STINKERBELL!

WHY SHOULD YOU NEVER SLEEP WITH YOUR HEAD UNDER THE PILLOW?

BECAUSE THE TOOTH FAIRY MIGHT TAKE ALL YOUR TEETH!

49

HOW DOES A WITCH TELL THE TIME?

SHE CHECKS HER WITCH-WATCH!

HOW DO LITTLE WITCHES LISTEN TO BEDTIME STORIES?

SPELLBOUND!

WHY DID THE WITCH DATE AN I.T. EXPERT?

SHE WANTED TO MARRY A COMPUTER WIZARD!

WHAT'S THE FIRST THING A WITCH READS IN A MAGAZINE?

HER HORROR-SCOPE!

WHAT DO YOU CALL A NERVOUS WITCH?

A TWITCH!

WHY DON'T WITCHES WEAR TOP HATS?

BECAUSE THERE'S NO POINT!

DID YOU HEAR ABOUT THE WITCHES WHO WERE IDENTICAL TWINS?

YOU COULDN'T TELL WHICH WITCH WAS WHICH!

DID YOU HEAR ABOUT THE WITCH WHO SNEEZED AND COUGHED?

IT WAS A COLD SPELL!

WHAT KIND OF PHONE DOES A MERMAID USE?

A SHELL PHONE!

WHY DID THE MERMAN HAVE HIS EARS TESTED?

HE THOUGHT HE MIGHT NEED A HERRING AID!

WHY DID THE MERMAN STOP READING A BOOK ABOUT AN ELECTRIC EEL?

IT WAS TOO SHOCKING!

WHAT SPORT DO MERMAIDS AND SEAHORSES PLAY?

WATER POLO!

HOW DOES AN OGRE COUNT TO TWELVE?

ON HIS FINGERS!

WHO GOES OUT WITH AN OGRE?

HIS GIRL-FIEND!

WHERE DO OGRES GO TO DANCE?

TO AN ODD-BALL!

WHAT DO YOU GIVE AN OGRE WITH ENORMOUS FEET?

PLENTY OF ROOM!

WHAT DO YOU GET IF YOU PUT A WIZARD AT THE NORTH POLE?

A COLD SPELL!

WHAT DID THE GOLDEN SNITCH SAY WHEN HARRY POTTER WAS BITTEN BY A MOSQUITO?

QUIDDITCHING!

WHAT DO YOU CALL A WIZARD FROM OUTER SPACE?

A FLYING SORCERER!

WHY DID THE WIZARD FLUNK SCHOOL?

HE WAS TERRIBLE AT SPELLING!

WHY DO DRAGONS SLEEP ALL DAY?

SO THEY CAN FIGHT KNIGHTS!

WHY DO DRAGONS LAY EGGS?

BECAUSE IF THEY DROPPED THEM, THEY WOULD BREAK!

WHAT SHOULD YOU DO WITH A GREEN DRAGON?

WAIT FOR IT TO RIPEN!

WHERE DO THE TOUGHEST DRAGONS COME FROM?

HARD-BOILED EGGS!

HOW DID JACK BREAK INTO THE GIANT'S CASTLE?

INTRUDER WINDOW!

WHERE DO YOU FIND A GIANT SCHOLAR?

AROUND THE NECK OF A GIANT'S SHIRT!

WHERE DO YOU FIND GIANT SNAILS?

ON A GIANT'S FINGERS!

WHAT WAS THE NAME OF THE GIANT'S GIRLFRIEND?

FIFI FO-FUM!

HOW DOES PERCY JACKSON CONTACT THE GODS?

HE CALLS THEM ON THE PERSEPHONE!

WHY WON'T YOU GET TO THE UNDERWORLD ON A RAINY DAY?

BECAUSE YOU HAVE TO MAKE HADES WHILE THE SUN SHINES!

HOW DID THE GREEK GOD KNOW WHICH TOOTHBRUSH TO USE?

THE HANDLES SAID, "HIS AND HERMES!"

HOW SHOULD YOU FEEL IF YOU MEET A THREE-HEADED DOG?

TERRIER-FIED!

69

WHAT DID THE WEREWOLF SAY WHEN IT STUBBED ITS TOE?

AOOOOOOOOWWWWW!

WHAT DAY DO WEREWOLVES LIKE THE BEST?

MOON-DAY!

WHAT'S THE BEST WAY TO GREET A WEREWOLF?

"HOWL DO YOU DO?"

WHAT DO YOU CALL A CREATURE THAT GETS LOST WHEN THERE'S A FULL MOON?

A WHERE-WOLF!

WHY DO WITCHES LOVE HOTELS?

THEY ALWAYS ORDER BROOM SERVICE!

WHY WAS THE WITCH LATE FOR SCHOOL?

BECAUSE SHE OVERSWEPT!

WHAT NOISE DOES A FLYING WITCH MAKE?

"BROOOOOOOOM!"

WHY DO WITCHES GET STIFF JOINTS?

THEY SUFFER FROM BROOMATISM!

DID YOU HEAR ABOUT THE MARRIED MAGICIANS WHO COULD MAKE THEMSELVES INVISIBLE?

THEIR KIDS WERE NOTHING TO LOOK AT EITHER!

DID YOU HEAR ABOUT THE MAGICIAN THAT THREW HIS WATCH UP IN THE AIR?

HE WANTED TO SEE TIME FLY!

DID YOU HEAR ABOUT THE MAGICIAN THAT LOST HIS TEMPER ON STAGE?

HE PULLED HIS HARE OUT!

DID YOU HEAR ABOUT THE MAGICIAN THAT DISAPPEARED DURING HIS ACT?

HE WAS GOING THROUGH A STAGE!

73

WHAT HAS SHARP
TEETH AND LIVES
AT THE END OF
THE RAINBOW?

THE CROC OF GOLD!

WHY DID
LITTLE
MISS
MUFFET
NEED
A MAP?

BECAUSE SHE'D
LOST HER WHEY!

WHY DID
RAPUNZEL GO
WILD AT PARTIES?

SHE LIKED TO LET
HER HAIR DOWN!

WHO TOLD THE
BIG, BAD WOLF
HE WAS UGLY
AND SMELLY?

LITTLE RUDE
RIDING HOOD!

WHAT SONG DO ELVES SING AT A THEME PARK?

"IT'S A SMALL WORLD!"

WHY DO ALL ELVES LOOK ALIKE?

BECAUSE THERE IS LITTLE DIFFERENCE BETWEEN THEM!

WHAT DO ELVES LEARN WHEN THEY START SCHOOL?

THEIR ELFABET!

WHY DID THE ELF STRUGGLE TO CONCENTRATE AT SCHOOL?

HE HAD A SHORT ATTENTION SPAN!

WHY DOESN'T HARRY POTTER'S GODFATHER LIKE PRACTICAL JOKES?

HE'S TOO SIRIUS!

WHY WAS HARRY POTTER GIVEN DETENTION?

HE WAS CURSING IN CLASS!

HOW DO YOU GET A MYTHICAL CREATURE INTO YOUR HOUSE?

THROUGH THE GRIFFIN-DOOR!

WHERE DO YOU FIND DUMBLEDORE'S ARMY?

UP HIS SLEEVY!

HOW DID HAGRID GET INTO HOGWARTS?

HE USED THE DUMBLE-DOOR!

WHY DOESN'T VOLDEMORT WEAR GLASSES?

NO ONE NOSE!

WHY IS MAD-EYE MOODY SUCH A BAD TEACHER?

HE CAN'T CONTROL HIS PUPILS!

HOW DOES HARRY POTTER CURE CHICKEN POX?

WITH QUIT-ITCH!

WHICH FISH COME OUT AT NIGHT?

STARFISH!

HOW DOES AN OCTOPUS MAKE A MERMAID LAUGH?

WITH TEN-TICKLES!

WHERE DO MERMAIDS WATCH MOVIES?

AT THE DIVE-IN!

WHY COULDN'T THE MERMAID TUNE IN HER RADIO?

SHE WAS ON THE WRONG WAVELENGTH!

DO YOU KNOW THE FAIRY TALE ABOUT THE FROG PRINCE?

REDDIT...

WHY DID GOLDILOCKS STIR THE PORRIDGE REALLY HARD?

BECAUSE DADDY BEAR TOLD HER TO BEAT IT!

WHAT DID HANSEL AND GRETEL SAY WHEN THEY BROKE THE WITCH'S HOUSE?

"THAT'S THE WAY THE COOKIE CRUMBLES!"

WHAT'S WOODEN, HAS A LONG NOSE, AND GOES BOING?

PINOCCHIO ON A BUNGEE JUMP!

DID YOU HEAR THE STORY ABOUT A MISERABLE BEAR?

IT WAS A GRIMM FURRY TALE!

WHAT'S THE TALE ABOUT AN INFECTED TOENAIL?

PUS IN BOOTS!

DID YOU HEAR THE STORY ABOUT THE PRINCESS WHO DRANK TOO MUCH JUICE?

IT'S CALLED THE PRINCESS AND THE PEE!

HAVE YOU HEARD THE STORY ABOUT A POOR LITTLE SPIDER?

IT'S CALLED SPINDERELLA!

WHAT DID THE WITCH DO WHEN HER BROOMSTICK BROKE?

SHE WITCH-HIKED!

WHO IS IN CHARGE OF THE LIGHTING AT HALLOWEEN?

THE LIGHTS WITCH!

WHY DON'T BAD-TEMPERED WITCHES RIDE BROOMSTICKS?

THEY'RE AFRAID OF FLYING OFF THE HANDLE!

WHAT DOES A WITCH BUY AT THE HAIRDRESSER'S?

SCARE SPRAY!

WHY DID LUCIUS MALFOY CROSS THE ROAD TWICE?

BECAUSE HE WAS A DOUBLE-CROSSER!

HOW DO DEATH EATERS FRESHEN THEIR BREATH?

WITH DEMENTOS!

WHAT KIND OF BREAKFAST CEREAL DO THEY SERVE AT HOGWARTS?

HUFFLEPUFFS!

WHAT DO YOU CALL QUIDDITCH PLAYERS WHO SHARE A DORM?

BROOM-MATES!

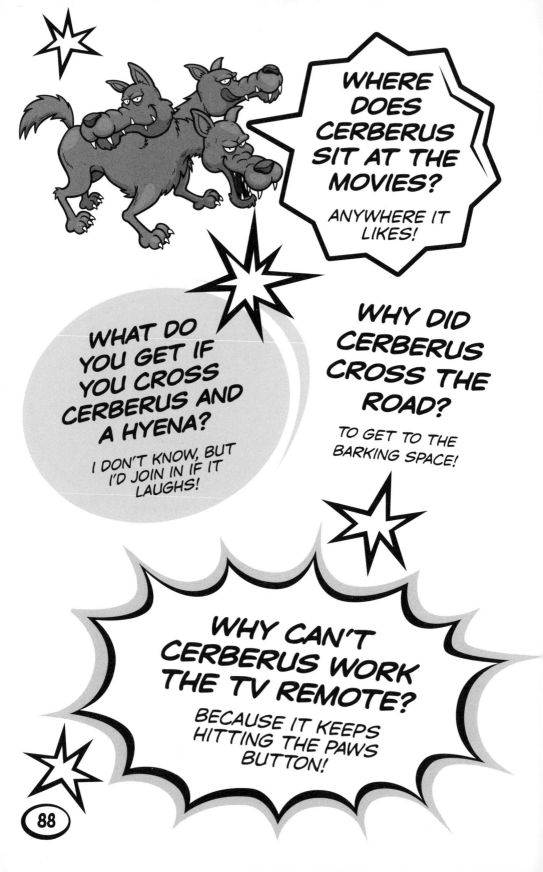

WHAT'S THE DIFFERENCE BETWEEN A STORM AND A HORSE?

ONE RAINS DOWN, THE OTHER IS REINED UP!

WHAT DID THE TORNADO SAY TO THE SPORTS CAR?

"WANT TO GO FOR A SPIN?"

WHAT KIND OF CLOTHES DO BLACK CLOUDS WEAR?

THUNDERWEAR!

WHAT'S THE DIFFERENCE BETWEEN A STORM CLOUD AND A BEAR RAIDING A BEEHIVE?

ONE POURS WITH RAIN AND THE OTHER ROARS WITH PAIN!

91

WHAT DOES A TREE WEAR TO A POOL PARTY?

SWIMMING TRUNKS!

HOW DO YOU DESCRIBE AN ACORN?

IN A NUTSHELL, IT'S AN OAK TREE!

WHAT KIND OF TREE CAN FIT INTO YOUR HAND?

A PALM TREE!

WHAT DID THE TREE DO WHEN THE LIBRARY WAS CLOSED?

IT TRIED ANOTHER BRANCH!

WHAT IS ON TOP OF A SNOWMAN'S BED?

A BLANKET OF SNOW!

WHAT DID THE POLAR BEAR SAY TO THE MELTING ICE?

"YOU NEED TO COOL DOWN!"

WHERE DO SNOWMEN UPLOAD THEIR WEBSITES?

ON THE WINTERNET!

WHAT HAPPENED TO THE SNOWMAN IN THE SPRING?

HE MADE A POOL OF HIMSELF!

WHY DID THE VULTURES ARGUE?

THEY HAD A BONE TO PICK WITH EACH OTHER!

WHERE DO TADPOLES CHANGE INTO FROGS?

IN THE CROAKROOM!

WHAT DO YOU CALL A MAN WHO LIVES WILD WITH A PACK OF WOLVES?

WOLFGANG!

WHAT LIVES IN THE FOREST AND REPEATS ITSELF?

A WILD BOAR.

WHAT KIND OF ANIMAL WILL NEVER OVERSLEEP?

A LLAMA CLOCK!

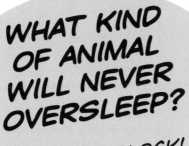

WHY IS IT HARD TO SPOT A CAMEL?

THEY ARE WELL CAMEL-FLAGED!

WHAT DO HORSES WEAR AT THE BEACH?

CLIP-CLOPS!

WHAT KIND OF ANIMAL IS BEST AT BREAK DANCING?

A HIP-HOP-POTAMUS!

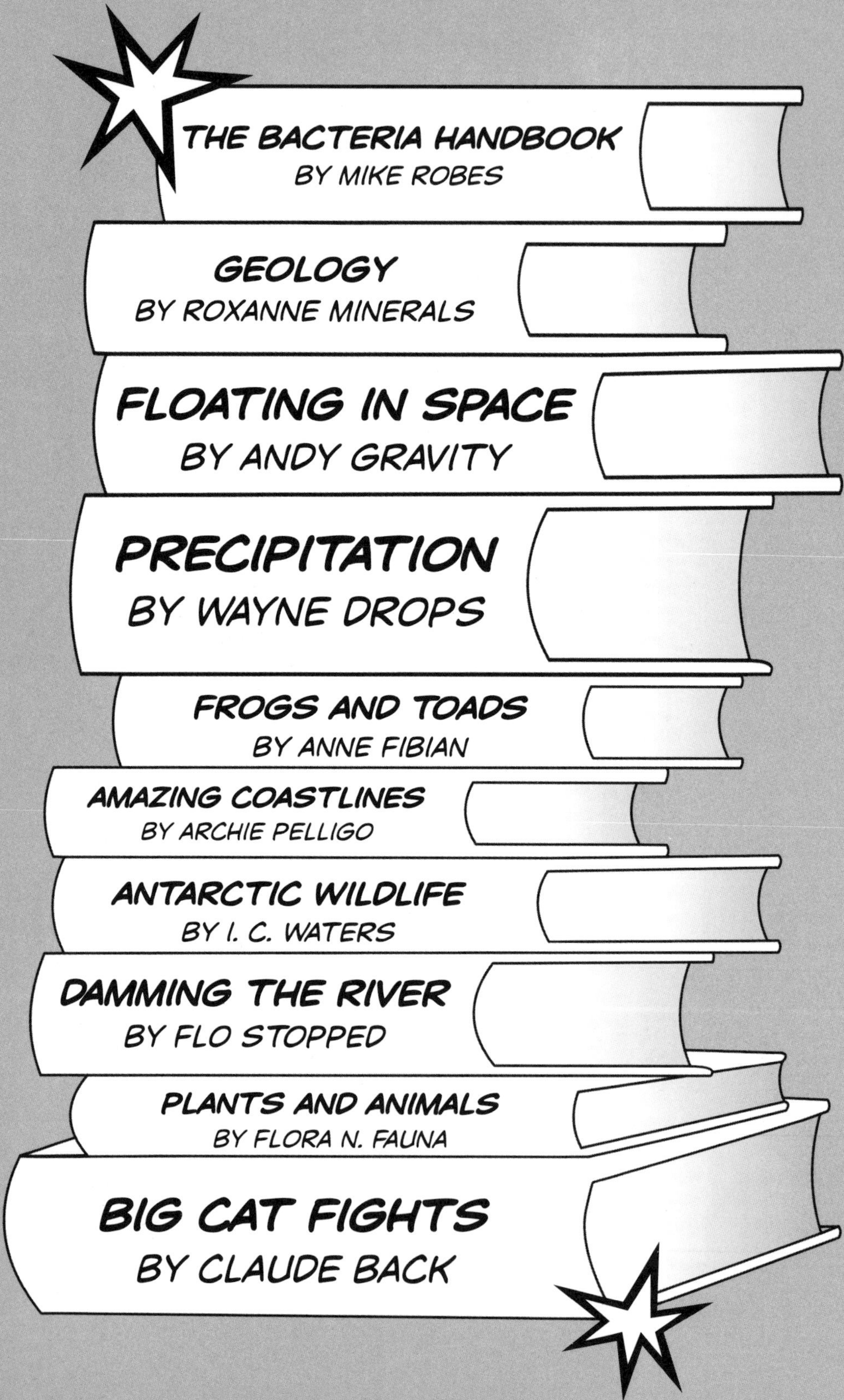
THE BACTERIA HANDBOOK
BY MIKE ROBES
GEOLOGY
BY ROXANNE MINERALS
FLOATING IN SPACE
BY ANDY GRAVITY
PRECIPITATION
BY WAYNE DROPS
FROGS AND TOADS
BY ANNE FIBIAN
AMAZING COASTLINES
BY ARCHIE PELLIGO
ANTARCTIC WILDLIFE
BY I. C. WATERS
DAMMING THE RIVER
BY FLO STOPPED
PLANTS AND ANIMALS
BY FLORA N. FAUNA
BIG CAT FIGHTS
BY CLAUDE BACK

WHAT DO YOU CALL A WOMAN WITH ONE LEG ON EITHER SIDE OF A RIVER?

BRIDGET!

WHAT DO YOU CALL A MAN WITH A SEAGULL ON HIS HEAD?

CLIFF!

WHAT DO YOU CALL A MAN WITH POCKETS FULL OF DRY LEAVES?

RUSSELL!

WHAT DO YOU CALL A GIRL WITH A FLOWER ON HER HEAD?

LILY!

WHERE DO WEATHERMEN GO FOR A DRINK?

THE CLOSEST ISOBAR!

WHAT DID ONE HURRICANE SAY TO THE OTHER?

"I HAVE MY EYE ON YOU!"

WHAT DO YOU SAY WHEN IT RAINS DUCKS AND CHICKENS?

"FOWL WEATHER, ISN'T IT?"

WHAT DID ONE TORNADO SAY TO THE OTHER?

"LET'S TWIST AGAIN LIKE WE DID LAST SUMMER!"

WHAT DID ONE RAINDROP SAY TO THE OTHER?

"TWO'S COMPANY, THREE'S A CLOUD!"

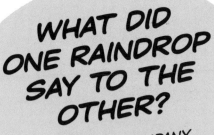

WHAT WAS THE WORST KIND OF WEATHER IN CAESAR'S DAYS?

ALL HAIL!

WHAT'S WORSE THAN RAINING CATS AND DOGS?

HAILING TAXIS!

DID YOU HEAR ABOUT THE HAPPY RAINDROP?

IT WAS ON CLOUD 9!

WHAT MONTH DO LUMBERJACKS LIKE THE BEST?

SEP-TIMBER!

WHY DO TREES HATE EXAMS?

THEY ARE EASILY STUMPED!

WHAT DID THE BEAVER SAY TO THE TREE?

"IT'S BEEN NICE GNAWING YOU!"

WHAT DID THE TREE SAY TO THE WOODPECKER?

"LEAF ME ALONE!"

WHY IS IT HARD TO WIND UP A SNAKE?

YOU CAN'T PULL ITS LEG!

WHY DIDN'T THE VIPER VIPER NOSE?

BECAUSE THE ADDER ADDER HANDKERCHIEF!

WHY COULDN'T THE SNAKE SAY ANYTHING?

IT HAD A FROG IN ITS THROAT!

DID YOU HEAR ABOUT THE SNAKE THAT WAS TRYING TO IMPRESS ITS DATE?

IT WAS A SNAKE CHARMER!

WHAT DID THE DIVER SHOUT WHEN HE SWAM INTO A SEAWEED FOREST?

"KELP!"

DO FISH LIKE TO WATCH BASEBALL?

YES–THERE ARE 20,000 LEAGUES UNDER THE SEA!

WHAT ARE LITTLE SEA CREATURES MOST AFRAID OF?

SQUID-NAPPERS!

WHY DO FISH IN A SCHOOL ALL SWIM IN THE SAME DIRECTION?

THEY'RE PLAYING SALMON SAYS!

WHAT DO YOU CALL A BIRD IN THE WINTER?

A BRRRRR-D!

HOW DO YOU CATCH A UNIQUE BIRD?

UNIQUE UP ON IT!

HOW DO YOU CATCH A TAME BIRD?

THE TAME WAY, UNIQUE UP ON IT!

WHAT DID THE BIRD SAY AS IT FINISHED BUILDING ITS NEST?

"THAT'S THE LAST STRAW!"

WHY ARE FROGS ALWAYS HAPPY?

BECAUSE THEY CAN EAT WHATEVER BUGS THEM!

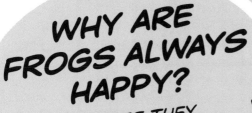

WHAT DID THE COW SAY WHEN IT WAS HUNGRY?

"THISTLE HAVE TO DO!"

WHAT DID THE SPIDER SAY WHEN ITS WEB GOT BROKEN?

"DARN IT!"

WHY DO MALE DEER NEED BRACES?

BECAUSE THEY HAVE BUCK TEETH!

CINDY: DID YOU KNOW IT'S RAINING CATS AND DOGS OUT THERE?

MINDY: I KNOW, I JUST STEPPED IN A POODLE!

WHAT'S THE DIFFERENCE BETWEEN WEATHER AND CLIMATE?

YOU CAN'T WEATHER A TREE, BUT YOU CAN CLIMATE!

WHY SHOULDN'T YOU ARGUE WITH A WEATHERMAN?

HE MIGHT STORM OUT ON YOU!

WHY DID THE MAN TAKE HIS WALLET OUT INTO THE STORM?

HE WAS HOPING FOR SOME CHANGE IN THE WEATHER!

WHAT DID THE WEATHER WOMAN USE TO CURL HER HAIR?

A HEAT WAVE!

WHY DID THE THERMOMETER GO TO COLLEGE?

TO GET A DEGREE!

DENNY: MY STUPID BROTHER TRIED TO CATCH FOG YESTERDAY.

LENNY: DON'T TELL ME – HE MIST?

DID YOU HEAR THAT DOROTHY AND TOTO GOT CAUGHT IN A STORM?

IT WAS THE BLIZZARD OF OZ!

WHY DID HUMPTY DUMPTY HAVE A GREAT FALL?

TO MAKE UP FOR A MISERABLE SUMMER!

WHAT DID THE BOY SAY AFTER READING FOR TOO LONG IN THE SUN?

"HMM, I'M CERTAINLY WELL RED!"

MAISIE: TEACHER SAYS WE'RE DOING OUR TEST TODAY, COME RAIN OR SHINE.

DAISY: YAY! IT'S SNOWING!

WHAT KIND OF WEATHER IS GOOD WHEN YOU'RE DINING OUT?

FORK LIGHTNING!

WHEN ARE YOUR EYES NOT YOUR EYES?

WHEN A COLD WIND MAKES THEM WATER!

WHEN DO MONKEYS FALL FROM THE SKY?

DURING APE-RIL SHOWERS!

WHAT DID THE KNITTED HAT SAY TO THE SCARF?

"YOU HANG AROUND WHILE I GO ON AHEAD!"

WHAT DID THE TREE SAY AFTER WINTER HAD PASSED?

WHAT A RE-LEAF!

WHAT DO ELEPHANTS DO WHEN IT RAINS?

THEY GET WET!

WHAT DOES AN OCTOPUS WEAR IN WINTER?

A COAT OF ARMS!

WHAT DO YOU CALL A BEAR IN WET WEATHER?

A DRIZZLY BEAR!

WHY DON'T OWLS DATE IN THUNDERSTORMS?

IT'S TOO WET TO WOO!

WHAT DO OAKS LEARN AT SCHOOL?

THEIR TREE TIMES TABLE!

HOW HARD IS IT TO COUNT SYCAMORES?

IT'S AS EASY AS ONE, TWO, TREE!

WHAT DID THE LEAF SAY WHEN IT FELL FROM THE TREE?

NOTHING, LEAVES DON'T TALK!

WHY AREN'T TREES GOOD AT QUIZZES?

BECAUSE THEY'RE OFTEN STUMPED!

HOW DO YOU GET RID OF AN ANNOYING WASP?

TELL IT TO BUZZ OFF!

WHAT GIFT DID THE SMELLY BEE RECEIVE FROM ITS FRIENDS?

BEE-ODORANT!

WHAT DO YOU CALL A BEE THAT IS UNHAPPY?

A GRUMBLEBEE!

DID YOU HEAR ABOUT THE BEE THAT SMELLED BAD?

IT HAD BEE-O!

WHAT GOES SNAP, CRACKLE, POP?

A FIREFLY WITH A SHORT CIRCUIT!

WHAT'S THE LARGEST MOTH IN THE WORLD?

A MAMMOTH!

WHAT DID THE WORM SAY TO HER SON WHEN HE CAME HOME LATE?

"WHERE IN EARTH HAVE YOU BEEN?"

WHAT DO YOU CALL A FLY WITH NO WINGS?

A WALK!

WHERE DO BEES GO WHEN THEY NEED TO USE THE BATHROOM?

THE BP STATION!

WHAT DO YOU CALL AN INTERFERING BEE?

A BUZZYBODY!

HOW CAN YOU TELL A WORM'S HEAD FROM ITS TAIL?

TICKLE THE MIDDLE, AND SEE WHICH END LAUGHS!

WHAT DID THE BEE SHOUT WHEN THE HIVE WAS UNDER ATTACK?

"BEE-WARE!"

FUNNY FAMILY

WHY WAS THE YOUNGEST OF SEVEN CHILDREN LATE FOR SCHOOL?

BECAUSE THE ALARM WAS SET FOR SIX!

TEACHER: WHAT IS THE PLURAL OF BABY?

FRANCES: TWINS!

TEACHER: DID YOUR MOTHER HELP YOU WITH YOUR HOMEWORK?

CHARLIE: NO, I GOT IT WRONG ALL BY MYSELF!

DAD: WHY DIDN'T YOU COME STRAIGHT HOME FROM SCHOOL?

SEBASTIAN: BECAUSE WE LIVE AROUND THE CORNER!

WHY DID DAD TAKE HIS RAZOR TO SPORTS DAY?

HE WANTED TO SHAVE A FEW SECONDS OFF HIS TIME!

EMILY: DAD, I GOT AN A IN SPELLING!

DAD: YOU FOOL, THERE ISN'T AN A IN SPELLING!

GRANDMA: I HEAR YOU'VE BEEN MISSING SCHOOL?

BRADLEY: THAT'S A LIE. I HAVEN'T MISSED IT ONE BIT!

DID YOU HEAR ABOUT THE EMBARRASSING TWINS IN THE LONG DISTANCE RACE?

ONE RAN IN SHORT BURSTS, THE OTHER RAN IN BURST SHORTS!

TILLY: MY AUNT HAS ONE LEG LONGER THAN THE OTHER.

BILLY: IS SHE CALLED EILEEN?

DAD, I CAN'T MOW THE LAWN TODAY, I'VE TWISTED MY ANKLE.

THAT'S A LAME EXCUSE!

WHY DID GRANDPA PUT WHEELS ON HIS ROCKING CHAIR?

HE WANTED TO ROCK AND ROLL!

DAD, I KEEP THINKING I'M A WOODWORM!

WELL, SON, LIFE DOES GET BORING SOMETIMES!

WHAT DO YOU GET IF YOU CROSS DAD'S SOCKS WITH A BOOMERANG?

A NASTY SMELL THAT KEEPS COMING BACK!

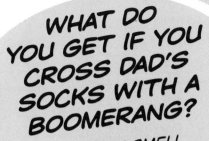

ANNIE: YOUR AUNT LOOKS SO OLD!

DANNY: YES, SHE'S AN AUNT-IQUE!

KATE: OUR MOTHER IS EXCELLENT AT HISTORY BUT AN AWFUL COOK.

NATE: I KNOW, SHE'S AN EXPERT ON ANCIENT GREASE!

WHY DOES YOUR SISTER PUT GLUE ON HER SALAD?

SHE WANTS TO STICK TO HER DIET!

MY BROTHER IS SO DUMB, HE FOUND THREE MILK CARTONS IN A FIELD AND THOUGHT IT WAS A COW'S NEST!

MY BROTHER IS SO DUMB, HE DRINKS HOT CHOCOLATE AT NIGHT SO HE WILL HAVE SWEET DREAMS!

MY BROTHER IS SO DUMB, HE THINKS GLUTEUS MAXIMUS IS A ROMAN EMPEROR!

MY BROTHER IS SO DUMB, HE WENT LOOKING FOR A HILLY LAKE SO HE COULD WATER SKI!

WHAT ANCIENT GREEK LAND IS LIKE YOUR BROTHER'S BEDROOM?

MESS-OPOTAMIA!

WHAT CLOTHES DOES A HOUSE WEAR?

ADDRESS!

WHAT DID THE ITALIAN SAY WHEN HE RETURNED FROM AN OVERSEAS TRIP?

"ROME, SWEET ROME!"

HOW MANY KIDS DOES IT TAKE TO CHANGE A LIGHT BULB?

THREE—ONE TO SAY, "BUT I DIDN'T LEAVE IT ON," AND TWO TO SAY, "BUT I CHANGED IT LAST TIME!"

WINNIE: WHY IS THERE A PLANE OUTSIDE YOUR BEDROOM DOOR?

VINNIE: I MUST HAVE LEFT THE LANDING LIGHT ON!

WHAT KIND OF MONSTER LIVES IN YOUR BROTHER'S ROOM?

THE LOCH MESS MONSTER!

JAN: HOW CAN YOU FIT TWENTY FRIENDS IN YOUR ROOM AT ONCE AND STILL PLAY A GAME?

STAN: WE'RE PLAYING SQUASH!

DAD: THERE'S A BURGLAR DOWNSTAIRS EATING THE CAKE YOUR SISTER BAKED.

HUGH: SHOULD I CALL THE POLICE OR AN AMBULANCE?

LITTLE SISTER: WHY IS OUR GOLDFISH ORANGE?

BIG BROTHER: BECAUSE THE WATER MAKES IT RUSTY!

DID YOU HEAR ABOUT THE GUPPY THAT WENT TO HOLLYWOOD?

IT BECAME A STARFISH!

KIM: WHY IS YOUR DRAWING OF A FISH SO TINY?

TIM: I'VE DRAWN IT TO SCALE!

WHAT IS STRANGER THAN SEEING A CAT FISH?

SEEING A GOLDFISH BOWL!

WHEN DOES A PET CAT GO "MOO?"

WHEN IT IS LEARNING A NEW LANGUAGE!

WHERE CAN YOU TAKE A PET CAT FOR A DAY TRIP?

TO THE MEW-SEUM!

WHAT DID THE CAT SAY TO THE FLEA?

"STOP BUGGING ME!"

WHAT IS IT CALLED WHEN YOUR PET CAT WINS A DOG SHOW?

A CAT-ASTROPHE!

DAD: YOU'VE BEEN WALKING SIDEWAYS EVER SINCE YOU CAME HOME FROM THE HOSPITAL.

HANNAH: THEY SAID MY MEDICINE MIGHT HAVE SIDE EFFECTS...

BOBBY: WHAT'S THE DIFFERENCE BETWEEN A HILL AND A PILL?

ROBBIE: A HILL IS HARD TO GET UP, BUT A PILL IS HARD TO GET DOWN.

WHAT DID THE MOTHER BROOM SAY TO HER SON?

IT'S TIME TO GO TO SWEEP!

WHAT CAN YOU GIVE AND KEEP AT THE SAME TIME?

A COLD!

CARRIE: HOW DID DAD GET AN INJURY ON A FISHING TRIP?

HARRY: HE PULLED A MUSSEL!

WHY DID THE HOUSE GO TO THE EMERGENCY ROOM?

BECAUSE IT HAD A WINDOW PANE!

MOTHER: YOU SHOULDN'T PLAY BALL TODAY, SON, YOU HAVE A SICKNESS BUG.

JIM: I KNOW, I KEEP THROWING UP!

STACEY: I WAS GIVEN X-RAYS BY MY DENTIST YESTERDAY.

CASEY: OH, TOOTH PICS?

MRS. SHARK: WHAT BOOK ARE YOU STUDYING AT SCHOOL, DEAR?

LITTLE SHARK: HUCKLEBERRY FIN!

HOW DID THE SHELLFISH KNOW HER KIDS WERE SICK?

THEY FELT CLAMMY!

WHY WAS THE BABY PANDA SO SPOILED?

BECAUSE ITS MOTHER PANDA-D TO ITS EVERY WHIM!

WHY WAS THE FROG WORRIED ABOUT HER SON?

BECAUSE HE LOOKED UNHOPPY!

147

WHAT DO YOU CALL A CAT THAT'S SWALLOWED A DUCK?

A DUCK-FILLED FATTY PUSS!

WHAT DO CATS PUT IN THEIR COLA?

UBES!

WHY ARE CATS SO GOOD AT PLAYING THE PIANO?

BECAUSE THEY ARE VERY MEW-SICAL!

WHO WON THE MILK-DRINKING COMPETITION?

THE CAT—IT LAPPED THE FIELD!

MY SISTER IS SO DUMB, SHE WENT TO THE DENTIST TO GET HER BLUETOOTH FIXED!

MY SISTER IS SO DUMB, SHE THOUGHT SPOTIFY WAS A STAIN REMOVER!

MY SISTER IS SO DUMB, SHE TRIED TO BUY TICKETS TO XBOX LIVE!

MY SISTER IS SO DUMB, SHE THOUGHT GOOSEBUMPS WERE TO STOP GEESE FROM SPEEDING!

WHAT HAPPENED TO THE MAN WHO PLUGGED HIS ELECTRIC BLANKET INTO THE TOASTER?

HE KEPT POPPING OUT OF BED ALL NIGHT!

WHAT DRESSING DO YOU PUT ON A SIMPLE SALAD?

CRUDE OIL!

DID YOU HEAR ABOUT THE CAT THAT SWALLOWED A BALL OF YARN?

SHE HAD MITTENS!

WHAT DO YOU GET IF YOU CROSS BAKED BEANS WITH ONIONS?

TEAR GAS!

WHEN SHOULD A MOUSE STAY INDOORS?

WHEN IT'S RAINING CATS AND DOGS!

WHO ARE SMALL, FURRY, AND FANTASTIC AT SWORD FIGHTING?

THE THREE MOUSEKETEERS!

WHY SHOULDN'T YOU WORRY IF YOU SEE MICE IN YOUR HOME?

THEY'RE PROBABLY DOING THE MOUSEWORK!

WHAT DO YOU DO IF YOUR PET MOUSE FALLS IN THE SINK?

GIVE IT MOUSE-TO-MOUSE RESUSCITATION!

CASEY: WHY IS YOUR SISTER SO GOOD AT SPORT?

STACEY: SHE HAS ATHLETE'S FOOT!

WHY DID THE JOGGER EAT ON THE RUN?

SHE LOVED FAST FOOD!

AMANDA: IS YOUR BROTHER ANY GOOD AT RUNNING?

MIRANDA: HE'S SO SLOW HE RAN A BATH AND CAME SECOND!

WHEN IS A BASKETBALL PLAYER LIKE A BABY?

WHEN HE DRIBBLES!

THELMA: IF THAT PLANET IS MARS, WHAT'S THE ONE HIGHER UP?

VELMA: IS IT PA'S?

FRED: MY TEACHER SAYS I SHOULD TRAIN TO BE AN ASTRONAUT.

JED: NO, SHE SAID YOU'RE A REAL SPACE CADET...

WHICH RELATIVE VISITS ASTRONAUTS IN OUTER SPACE?

AUNTIE GRAVITY!

WHY ARE GRANDPA'S TEETH LIKE STARS?

BECAUSE THEY COME OUT AT NIGHT!

DAD: WHAT HAPPENED TO YOUR AMAZING FIVE-DAY DIET?

EDWARD: I FINISHED ALL THE FOOD IN TWO DAYS!

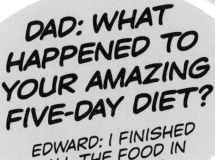

DREW: IF CAN'T IS SHORT FOR CANNOT, WHAT IS DON'T SHORT FOR?

SUE: DONUT?

WHAT'S THE DIFFERENCE BETWEEN A BORING PARENT AND A BORING BOOK?

YOU CAN SHUT THE BOOK UP!

DEAN: CAN WE WATCH THE CURSE OF THE BLACK PEARL TONIGHT?

JEAN: DAD WON'T LET US WATCH PIRATE DVDS.

ALAN: IS MY SUPPER READY? I HAVE KARATE CLASS IN AN HOUR.

MOTHER: YOUR CHOPS ARE ON THE TABLE!

EDWIN: I DON'T LIKE CHEESE WITH HOLES!

DAD: WELL, EAT THE CHEESE AND LEAVE THE HOLES ON THE SIDE OF YOUR PLATE.

WHY DID THE GIRL STARE AT THE CARTON OF ORANGE JUICE?

IT SAID "CONCENTRATE."

GRANDMA: EAT YOUR GREENS, THEY'RE GOOD FOR YOUR SKIN.

ALICE: BUT I DON'T WANT GREEN SKIN!

160

MY COUSIN IS SO DUMB, SHE WENT TO THE LIBRARY TO FIND FACEBOOK!

MY COUSIN IS SO DUMB, HE LOOKED ON A MAP FOR MOUNTAIN DEW!

MY COUSIN IS SO DUMB, HE TOOK HIS COMPUTER TO THE NURSE BECAUSE IT HAD A VIRUS!

MY COUSIN IS SO DUMB, HE WENT TO BUY SOME CAMOUFLAGE PANTS BUT COULDN'T FIND ANY!

LITTLE PENCIL:
YOU LOOK AS
THOUGH YOU'VE PUT
ON WEIGHT, DAD.

DADDY PENCIL:
YOU'RE VERY BLUNT!

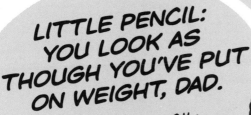

WHY WAS
THE LITTLE
BROOM
LATE FOR
SCHOOL?

IT
OVERSWEPT!

WHY WAS
THE LITTLE
ICEBERG JUST
LIKE HIS DAD?

BECAUSE HE WAS
A CHIP OFF THE
COLD BLOCK!

WHAT DID THE
MOTHER DOG SAY TO
THE PUPPY?

"WE'RE HAVING DINNER
SOON, DON'T EAT TOO MUCH
HOMEWORK!"

CLARK: WHY IS YOUR GRANDPA DRESSED AS A CLOWN?

MARK: JEST FOR FUN!

HOW DO YOU MAKE ANTIFREEZE?

HIDE HER COAT AND GLOVES!

MICKEY: OUR MOTHER HAS NAMED US ALL AFTER MEMBERS OF OUR FAMILY.

NICKY: IS THAT WHY YOUR BIG BROTHER IS CALLED UNCLE JOE?

DID YOU HEAR THAT UNCLE BOB LOST HIS WIG ON THE ROLLER COASTER?

IT WAS A HAIR-RAISING RIDE!

WHY DO LITTLE KIDS LISTEN TO THE RADIO ON LONG TRIPS?

BECAUSE CAR-TOONS KEEP THEM HAPPY!

JOSIE: MY SINGING TUTOR SAID MY VOICE IS HEAVENLY!

ROSIE: NOT REALLY – SHE SAID IT WAS LIKE NOTHING ON EARTH!

DID YOU HEAR ABOUT THE MAGICIAN WHO TRIED HIS SAWING-A-PERSON-IN-TWO TRICKS AT HOME?

HE HAD LOTS OF HALF BROTHERS AND SISTERS!

MOTHER: WHY DID YOU KICK YOUR BROTHER IN THE STOMACH?

SALLY: IT WAS AN ACCIDENT – HE TURNED AROUND!

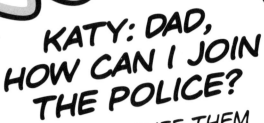

KATY: DAD, HOW CAN I JOIN THE POLICE?

DAD: HANDCUFF THEM ALL TOGETHER!

MATT: WHY DID YOUR DAD QUIT HIS JOB AT THE CAN CRUSHING PLANT?

KAT: BECAUSE IT WAS SODA PRESSING!

CHRIS: MY DAD'S AN UNDERTAKER.

FLISS: DOES HE ENJOY IT?

CHRIS: OF CORPSE HE DOES!

GRANDMA: WHAT DO YOU WANT TO BE WHEN YOU GROW UP, DEAR?

NATHANIEL: I'M ASPIRIN' TO BE A PHARMACIST!

CARRIE: DID YOU JUST FEED GARLIC BREAD TO OUR DOG?

HARRY: YES–ITS BARK IS MUCH WORSE THAN ITS BITE!

DANNY: MA, SHE'S STOLEN THE YOLK FROM MY EGG!

ANNIE: SHH, IT'S ALL WHITE NOW!

DAD: WHY DO YOUR SHOES LOOK LIKE BANANAS?

HARRIET: THEY'RE MY SLIPPERS!

MOTHER: WHAT DO IDK, LY AND TTYL MEAN?

DAUGHTER: I DON'T KNOW, LOVE YOU, TALK TO YOU LATER.

MOTHER: WELL, I'LL HAVE TO ASK YOUR SISTER THEN!

WHAT DO YOU GET IF YOU CROSS A DOG AND A FROG?

A PET THAT CAN LICK YOU FROM THE OTHER SIDE OF THE ROAD!

WHAT INSTRUMENT DO DOGS LIKE BEST?

THE TROM-BONE!

WHAT DO YOU GET IF YOU CROSS A COCKER SPANIEL, A POODLE, AND A ROOSTER?

COCKERPOODLEDOO!

WHAT HAPPENED TO THE DOG THAT SWALLOWED A FIREFLY?

IT BARKED WITH DE-LIGHT!

DAD: WHY DID YOU OVERSLEEP THIS MORNING?

TOBY: I WAS DREAMING ABOUT PLAYING FOOTBALL, AND IT WENT INTO EXTRA TIME!

NED: WHY IS THE LIGHT ALWAYS ON IN YOUR BROTHER'S ROOM?

FRED: BECAUSE HE'S SO DIM!

DAD: HAVE YOU HAD YOUR HOMEWORK MARKED YET?

BECKY: YES, I'M AFRAID YOU DIDN'T DO VERY WELL!

FLO: WHY ARE YOU CRYING AND CHEWING AT THE SAME TIME?

JOE: I JUST SWALLOWED SOME BLUBBER GUM!

CHLOE: HOW COME YOU'RE SO GOOD AT TENNIS?

ZOE: IT'S NOT RACKET SCIENCE!

MARK: WHY HAVE YOU VOLUNTEERED FOR HIGH JUMP FOR THE FIRST TIME EVER?

CLARK: I THOUGHT I MIGHT DO WELL AS IT'S A LEAP YEAR!

FLORENCE: WHY DO YOU ONLY PLAY BASEBALL AT NIGHT?

I HAVE A VAMPIRE BAT!

BOBBY: WHAT POSITION DOES YOUR BROTHER PLAY ON THE TEAM?

ROBBIE: I THINK HE'S ONE OF THE DRAWBACKS!

HOW DID VIKINGS SEND SECRET MESSAGES?

THEY USED NORSE CODE!

WHY DID THE VIKING NEED CHEERING UP?

HE HAD A SINKING FEELING.

WHERE DID THE TEACHER SEND THE VIKING WHEN HE GOT SICK IN CLASS?

TO THE SCHOOL NORSE!

WHEN DID THE VIKINGS MAKE THEIR RAIDS?

DURING A PLUNDER STORM!

WHAT HAPPENED TO THE ROYAL CHICKEN THAT COULDN'T LAY EGGS?
THE KING HAD HER EGGS-ECUTED!

WHY DID THE KING VISIT THE DENTIST?
TO HAVE HIS TEETH CROWNED!

WHAT DID KING HENRY VIII DO WHENEVER HE BURPED?
HE ISSUED A ROYAL PARDON!

WHY DID EVERYONE IN 19TH-CENTURY ENGLAND CARRY AN UMBRELLA?
BECAUSE QUEEN VICTORIA'S REIGN LASTED FOR 64 YEARS!

WHAT WAS THE FIRST THING QUEEN VICTORIA DID ON ASCENDING TO THE THRONE?

SAT DOWN!

WHAT DO YOU CALL IT WHEN THE QUEEN GOES TO THE BATHROOM?

A ROYAL FLUSH!

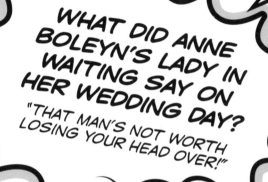

WHAT DID ANNE BOLEYN'S LADY IN WAITING SAY ON HER WEDDING DAY?

"THAT MAN'S NOT WORTH LOSING YOUR HEAD OVER!"

WHY DID THEY CALL KING ALFRED "THE GREAT?"

BECAUSE ALFRED THE FANTASTIC SOUNDED WRONG!

179

WHY COULDN'T THE ANIMALS PLAY CARDS ON NOAH'S ARK?

BECAUSE NOAH WAS STANDING ON THE DECK!

HOW DID NOAH NAVIGATE IN THE DARK?

HE USED FLOODLIGHTS!

WHAT DID NOAH DO FOR A LIVING?

HE WAS AN ARK-ITECT!

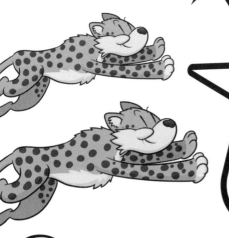

WHAT HAPPENED WHEN THEY FINALLY GOT THE CARDS ON NOAH'S ARK?

THEIR GAME WAS RUINED BY TWO CHEETAHS!

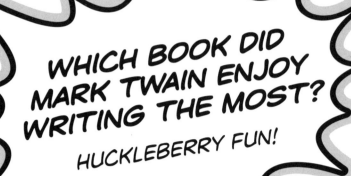

WHICH BOOK DID MARK TWAIN ENJOY WRITING THE MOST?

HUCKLEBERRY FUN!

HOW DID THE HUNCHBACK OF NOTRE DAME CURE HIS SORE THROAT?

HE GARGOYLED!

HOW DID NEIL ARMSTRONG SAY HE WAS SORRY?

HE APOLLO-GIZED!

WHAT DO YOU CALL A FORTUNATE DETECTIVE?

SHEERLUCK HOLMES!

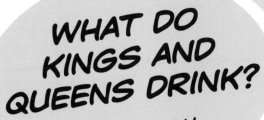

WHAT DO KINGS AND QUEENS DRINK?

ROYAL-TEA!

WHICH GORILLA HAD SIX WIVES?

HENRY THE APE!

WHAT WAS QUEEN VICTORIA'S MOST TREASURED ITEM OF CLOTHING?

HER REIGN-COAT!

WHAT DID QUEEN VICTORIA SAY WHEN SHE STEPPED IN COW DUNG?

"WE ARE NOT A-MOO-SED!"

WHY DID AL CAPONE FIRE HIS CLEANER?

HE WANTED TO BE A FAMOUS GRIME LORD!

WHO IS THE HEAD OF THE UNDERWATER CRIME RING?

THE CODFATHER!

WHO WAS THE MOST FEARED GUNFIGHTER IN THE OCEAN?

BILLY THE SQUID!

WHY WAS AL CAPONE BEST FRIENDS WITH A FISHERMAN?

THEY GOT ALONG BY HOOK OR BY CROOK!

WHO RIDES A HORSE, WEARS A MASK, AND SMELLS GOOD?

THE COLOGNE RANGER!

WHAT DO YOU CALL A FROG WHO WANTS TO BE A COWBOY?

HOPPALONG CASSIDY!

MR. MONEY: I ASKED MY CLASS TO NAME A CREATURE THAT WAS HALF-MAN AND HALF-BEAST.

MR. HONEY: SO DID I. THEY SAID BUFFALO BILL.

WHY DID THE COWBOY CHOOSE HIS HORSE IN DAYTIME?

HE DIDN'T WANT NIGHTMARES!

WHY WAS IT CALLED THE DARK AGES?
BECAUSE THERE WERE SO MANY KNIGHTS!

WHAT WAS WRITTEN ON THE KNIGHT'S TOMB?
RUST IN PEACE!

WHAT WAS CAMELOT FAMOUS FOR?
ITS KNIGHT LIFE!

HOW DO YOU INTERRUPT A KNIGHT?
"JOUST A MINUTE...!"

WHAT DID THE COLONISTS WEAR AT THE BOSTON TEA PARTY?

TEA-SHIRTS!

WHY DIDN'T GEORGE WASHINGTON BOTHER GOING TO BED?

BECAUSE HE COULDN'T LIE!

WHAT KIND OF TEA WERE THE COLONISTS LOOKING FOR?

LIBER-TEA!

WHERE DID THE PILGRIMS LAND WHEN THEY ARRIVED IN AMERICA?

ON THE BEACH!

WHY DOES THE STATUE OF LIBERTY STAND IN NEW YORK?

BECAUSE IT CAN'T SIT DOWN!

WHO SUCCEEDED THE FIRST PRESIDENT OF THE UNITED STATES?

THE SECOND ONE!

WHERE WAS THE DECLARATION OF INDEPENDENCE SIGNED?

AT THE BOTTOM!

WHY WAS ABRAHAM LINCOLN BURIED IN SPRINGFIELD, ILLINOIS?

BECAUSE HE WAS DEAD!

WHAT DO YOU GET IF YOU CROSS A ROMAN EMPEROR WITH A BOA CONSTRICTOR?

JULIUS SQUEEZER!

WHO WOULD REFEREE A TENNIS MATCH BETWEEN JULIUS CAESAR AND BRUTUS?

A ROMAN UMPIRE!

WHICH ROMAN EMPEROR WAS THE COOLEST?

JULIUS FREEZER!

WHICH ROMAN EMPEROR WAS ASTHMATIC?

JULIUS WHEEZER!

WHY DID CAVEMEN LOVE TO EAT SLOTHS?

THEY KNEW THAT FAST FOOD WAS BAD FOR YOU!

HOW DID CAVEMEN DRESS IN THE SNOW?

QUICKLY!

TEACHER: WHAT CAME AFTER THE STONE AGE AND THE BRONZE AGE?

ADRIAN: THE SAUS-AGE?

WHAT SWEET TREAT DID CAVEMEN LIKE THE BEST?

SPEARMINTS!

WHAT DO HISTORY TEACHERS DO ON A DATE?

TALK ABOUT THE GOOD OLD DAYS!

WHY IS HISTORY SUCH A SWEET SUBJECT?

BECAUSE IT'S FULL OF DATES!

HOW DID PEOPLE TIE THEIR SHOELACES IN THE MIDDLE AGES?

WITH A LONG BOW!

WHY DID ANCIENT CIVILIZATIONS HAVE NICE, SMOOTH CLOTHES?

THEY LIVED IN THE IRON AGE!

TEACHER: CAN YOU THINK OF AN ANCIENT MUSICAL INSTRUMENT?

JAKE: AN ANGLO-SAXOPHONE?

WHICH MONARCH HAD THE WORST SKIN?

MARY QUEEN OF SPOTS!

DID YOU HEAR ABOUT THE QUEEN WHOSE ELDEST SON DISOBEYED HER?

SHE WAS HAVING A BAD HEIR DAY!

DAWN: I WISH I'D BEEN BORN 500 YEARS AGO.

SHAUN: WHY'S THAT?

DAWN: SO I WOULDN'T HAVE TO LEARN SO MUCH HISTORY!

WHAT DOES AN EXECUTIONER READ IN THE MORNING?

THE NOOSE-PAPER!

WHAT DID THE EXECUTIONER SAY TO THE PRISONER?

"TIME TO HEAD OFF!"

WHAT DID THE EXECUTIONER SHOUT TO THE LINE OF PRISONERS?

"NECKS, PLEASE!"

WHAT DO YOU GET IF YOU CROSS A HANGMAN AND A CIRCUS PERFORMER?

SOMEONE WHO GOES STRAIGHT FOR THE JUGGLER!

WHY DID THE ARCHER CHANGE HIS CAREER?

HE FOUND HIS JOB TOO ARROWING!

WHAT WOULD YOU GET HANGING FROM CASTLE WALLS?

TIRED ARMS!

WHY DID THE HANGMAN'S WIFE ASK FOR A DIVORCE?

HER HUSBAND WAS A PAIN IN THE NECK!

WHY DID SOLDIERS FIRE ARROWS FROM THE CASTLE?

THEY WERE TRYING TO GET THEIR POINT ACROSS!

WHY DID THE SOLDIER SALUTE A TIGER?

IT HAD MORE STRIPES!

WHY DID THE SOLDIER PUT A TANK IN HIS HOUSE?

IT WAS A FISH TANK!

DID YOU HEAR ABOUT THE KARATE CHAMPION WHO JOINED THE ARMY?

THE FIRST TIME HE SALUTED, HE KNOCKED HIMSELF OUT!

MAJOR: I DIDN'T SEE YOU IN CAMOUFLAGE TRAINING THIS MORNING, PRIVATE!

PRIVATE: THANK YOU VERY MUCH, SIR!

WHY DID THE ROMANS BUILD SUCH STRAIGHT ROADS?

SO THEIR SOLDIERS DIDN'T GO AROUND THE BEND!

WHAT DO YOU SAY TO GET ROMANS TO SING ALONG?

"ALL TOGA-ETHER NOW!"

NERO: WHAT TIME IS IT?

SERVANT: X PAST V!

WHAT DO YOU CALL A ROMAN EMPEROR WHO HAS ADVENTURES?

AN ACTION NERO!

WHY IS IT NO FUN BEING AN ARCHEOLOGIST?

THEIR CAREER IS ALWAYS IN RUINS!

WHY WAS IT HOT INSIDE THE COLISEUM?

BECAUSE OF ALL THE GLADI-RADIATORS!

HOW WAS THE ROMAN EMPIRE DIVIDED UP?

WITH A PAIR OF CAESARS!

WHAT IS A FORUM?

TWO-UM PLUS TWO-UM!

WHICH ENGLISHMAN INVENTED FRACTIONS?

HENRY THE EIGHTH!

WHO INVENTED MATCHES?

SOME BRIGHT SPARK!

WHAT HAPPENED WHEN THE WHEEL WAS INVENTED?

IT CAUSED A REVOLUTION!

WHAT HAPPENED WHEN ELECTRICITY WAS FIRST DISCOVERED?

PEOPLE GOT A NASTY SHOCK!

WHICH ANIMAL INVENTED THE INTERNET?

THE BEAVER, SINCE IT WAS THE FIRST TO LOG ON!

WHAT INVENTION LETS YOU SEE THROUGH WALLS?

THE WINDOW!

WHAT WAS THE NAME OF THE INVENTOR OF THE COMPUTER?

CHIP!

WHAT WAS THE FIRST THING SAID BY THE INVENTOR OF THE STINK BOMB?

"YOU REEK, UGH!"

WHY WAS THE PHARAOH SO TENSE?

HE WAS GETTING WOUND UP!

WHY DID THE MUMMY CALL THE DOCTOR?

BECAUSE HE WAS COFFIN!

WHAT KIND OF JEWELS DID THE ANCIENT EGYPTIANS DECORATE THEIR COFFINS WITH?

TOMB-STONES!

DID YOU HEAR ABOUT THE MUMMY THAT LOST ITS TEMPER?

IT FLIPPED ITS LID!

211

WHICH ANCIENT GREEK WAS THE BEST OF THE BUNCH?

ALEXANDER THE GRAPE!

WHY WAS THE BULLHEADED CREATURE NOT ALLOWED TO VOTE?

BECAUSE IT WAS ONLY A MINOR-TAUR!

WHICH FRUIT LAUNCHED A THOUSAND SHIPS?

MELON OF TROY!

WHAT MOVIE DID THE ANCIENT GREEKS LIKE BEST?

TROY STORY!

WHAT DID ONE AZTEC SAY TO ANOTHER?

WE ALL HAVE TO MAKE SACRIFICES!

WHY DID SIR WALTER RALEIGH SAIL TO SOUTH AMERICA?

IT WAS TOO FAR TO SWIM!

WHERE DID MONTEZUMA GO TO COLLEGE?

AZ TECH!

WHEN DID MONTEZUMA DIE?

A FEW DAYS BEFORE THEY BURIED HIM!

WHY WERE THE DARK AGES SO CONFUSING?

IT WAS COMMON TO HEAR, "GOOD MORNING, GOOD KNIGHT!"

SHIRLEY: WHEN WAS THE MAGNA CARTA SIGNED?

HURLEY: 1215.

SHIRLEY: OH, JUST BEFORE LUNCH THEN!

WHY WERE BRITISH PEOPLE REALLY TANNED OVER 2,000 YEARS AGO?

THEY LIVED IN THE BRONZED AGE!

WHAT WAS IN FASHION AT THE TIME OF THE GREAT FIRE OF LONDON?

BLAZERS!

SILLY
CELEBRATIONS

WHY DID THE SCIENTIST USE A MICROSCOPE TO READ HIS VALENTINE CARD?

BECAUSE IT WAS VALEN-TINY!

WHY DO SKUNKS LOVE VALENTINE'S DAY?

BECAUSE THEY'RE SCENT-IMENTAL!

WHAT DID THE RECTANGLE WRITE IN THE TRIANGLE'S VALENTINE?

"I THINK YOU'RE ACUTE!"

HOW DID THE SKELETON KNOW HE HAD FOUND TRUE LOVE?

HE FELT IT IN HIS BONES!

WHAT SORT OF JOKES DO EASTER CHICKS LIKE?

CORNY ONES!

WHERE DO YOU FIND THE BEST EASTER EGG JOKES?

IN A YOLK BOOK!

WHAT KIND OF PEOPLE ARE THE BEST AT EASTER EGG HUNTS?

EGGSPLORERS!

WHAT DID THE EASTER BUNNY SAY TO THE CARROT?

"IT'S BEEN NICE GNAWING YOU!"

WHY CAN'T YOU TAKE A TURKEY TO CHURCH?

BECAUSE THEY USE SUCH FOWL LANGUAGE!

WHEN DOES CHRISTMAS COME BEFORE THANKSGIVING?

IN THE DICTIONARY!

WHAT SMELLS THE BEST AT A THANKSGIVING DINNER?

YOUR NOSE!

WHAT SHOULD YOU WEAR TO THANKSGIVING DINNER?

A HAR-VEST!

WHAT DO MATHEMATICIANS EAT FOR THANKSGIVING DINNER?

PUMPKIN PI!

WHY ARE TURKEYS WISER THAN CHICKENS?

EVER HEARD OF KENTUCKY FRIED TURKEY?!

WHY DID THE TURKEY WANT TO JOIN A BAND?

BECAUSE HE ALREADY HAD THE DRUMSTICKS!

WHAT DID THE TURKEY SAY WHEN IT SAW THE FARMER?

"QUACK, QUACK!"

WHERE IS THE BEST PLACE TO GO ON HALLOWEEN?

THE SCREAM PARK!

WHICH RIDE DO GHOSTS ENJOY THE MOST?

THE ROLLER GHOSTER!

WHERE IN A HAUNTED HOUSE WILL YOU AVOID ALL THE GHOSTS?

THE LIVING ROOM!

WHY DIDN'T THE GHOST TRY TO WIN A CUDDLY TOY?

HE DIDN'T HAVE A GHOST OF A CHANCE!

225

WHO DRESSES IN RED AND WHITE, AND IS A DANGER IN THE WATER?

SANTA JAWS!

HOW MUCH DID SANTA PAY FOR HIS SLEIGH?

NOTHING, IT WAS ON THE HOUSE!

WHAT DO SNOWMEN SING TO SANTA CLAUS?

"FREEZE A JOLLY GOOD FELLOW!"

WHAT DO YOU SHOUT WHEN SANTA TAKES THE ROLL CALL?

"PRESENT!"

WHAT DO
REINDEER HANG ON
THEIR CHRISTMAS
TREES?

HORN-AMENTS!

WHAT DO
GHOSTS
PUT ON
THEIR
TURKEY AT
CHRISTMAS?

GRAVE-Y!

WHAT
SNEAKS AROUND
THE KITCHEN ON
CHRISTMAS EVE?

MINCE SPIES!

WHAT CAN YOU
SEE FLYING THROUGH
THE SKY ON
CHRISTMAS EVE?

A U.F. HO-HO-HO!

WHAT DID THE BOA CONSTRICTOR WRITE IN ITS VALENTINE CARD?

"I HAVE A CRUSH ON YOU!"

WHAT SONG DOES A BULL SING ON VALENTINE'S DAY?

"WHEN I FALL IN LOVE...IT WILL BE FOR HEIFER."

WHAT DID ONE STAR SAY TO ANOTHER STAR?

"DO YOU WANT TO GLOW ON A DATE?"

WHAT DID THE NEEDLE SAY TO THE BUTTON?

"I LOVE YOU SEW MUCH!"

WHY WAS THE CHICKEN STRESSED?

BECAUSE SHE'D MISLAID HER EGGS!

WHEN IS THE BEST TIME TO BUY EASTER CHICKS?

WHEN THEY'RE GOING CHEEP!

IN WHICH DIRECTION DO YOU HEAD TO FIND CHOCOLATE EGGS?

A LITTLE EASTER HERE!

WHY DID THE EASTER BUNNY WANT TO MOVE?

HE WAS FED UP OF THE HOLE THING!

WHAT DID THE WOODCUTTER'S WIFE SAY TO HER HUSBAND ON DECEMBER 1ST?

"NOT MANY CHOPPING DAYS LEFT UNTIL CHRISTMAS!"

HOW DID JACK FROST BREAK HIS WRIST?

HE FELL OFF HIS ICICLE!

HAVE YOU HEARD THE SILLY STORY ABOUT A GIANT MINCE PIE?

IT'S VERY HARD TO SWALLOW.

WHO DELIVERS PRESENTS TO PETS?

SANTA CLAWS!

WHAT DO ANGRY MICE SEND EACH OTHER AT CHRISTMAS?

CROSS-MOUSE CARDS!

WHAT DO YOU GET IF YOU CROSS AN APPLE WITH A CHRISTMAS TREE?

A PINEAPPLE!

DOCTOR, I CAN'T SLEEP BECAUSE I AM SO EXCITED ABOUT CHRISTMAS!

LIE ON THE EDGE OF YOUR BED, AND YOU'LL SOON DROP OFF!

WHAT DOES MOWGLI SING AT CHRISTMAS?

"JUNGLE BELLS, JUNGLE BELLS..."

WHAT DID ONE SNOWMAN SAY TO THE OTHER?

"CAN YOU SMELL CARROTS?"

WHAT DO YOU GET IN DECEMBER THAT YOU DON'T GET IN ANY OTHER MONTH?

THE LETTER D!

HOW DOES GOOD KING WENCESLAS LIKE HIS PIZZA?

DEEP PAN, CRISP, AND EVEN!

WHAT'S WHITE AND GOES UP?

A STUPID SNOWFLAKE!

WHAT WAS THE CHEF'S SECRET INGREDIENT FOR LOVE?

VALEN-THYME!

DID YOU HEAR ABOUT THE COUPLE WHO MET IN A REVOLVING DOOR?

THEY'RE STILL GOING AROUND TOGETHER!

WHAT MESSAGE WAS INSIDE THE RABBIT'S VALENTINE CARD?

SOME BUNNY LOVES YOU!

WHAT DID THE PIG FARMER GIVE HIS WIFE ON VALENTINE'S DAY?

HOGS AND KISSES!

WHY DID THE EASTER BUNNY GET ARRESTED?

HE WAS CHARGED WITH HARE-ASSMENT!

HOW DOES THE EASTER BUNNY KEEP HIS FUR NEAT?

WITH A HARE BRUSH!

WHERE DO SHEEP KEEP THEIR EASTER EGGS?

IN A BAA-SKET!

WHAT DO YOU GIVE TO AN EASTER CHICK WITH A COLD?

A HEN-KERCHIEF!

WHY DON'T SKELETONS LIKE THANKSGIVING?

THEY HAVEN'T ANY BODY TO SPEND IT WITH!

WHAT DO VAMPIRES SING ON NEW YEAR'S EVE?

AULD FANG SYNE!

WHY DIDN'T THE SKELETON TELL HIS VALENTINE HE LOVED HER?

HE DIDN'T HAVE THE GUTS!

WHEN DO GHOSTS PLAY TRICKS ON EACH OTHER?

APRIL GHOUL'S DAY!

WHAT MONSTER PLAYS TRICKS ON HALLOWEEN?

PRANK-ENSTEIN!

WHAT DO GHOULS PUT ON THEIR BAGELS?

SCREAM CHEESE!

WHAT DID THE UNHAPPY GHOST SAY?

"BOO-HOO!"

WHAT DO YOU CALL A NATIVE AMERICAN GHOST?

POCA-HAUNT-US!

WHY DID THE GHOST GO UP THE STAIRS?

TO RAISE ITS SPIRITS!

WHAT DOES A SHORT-SIGHTED GHOST NEED?

SPOOK-TACLES!

WHAT CAN YOU HEAR AT HALLOWEEN SAYING, "BITE, SLURP, OUCH!"?

A VAMPIRE WITH A TOOTHACHE!

WHY COULDN'T THE GHOST FIND ITS DAD?

BECAUSE HE WAS TRANSPARENT!

WHAT FRUIT DO VAMPIRES LOVE?

NECK-TARINES!

WHO HAS FANGS AND WEBBED FEET?

COUNT QUACKULA!

WHY DO VAMPIRES NEED MOUTHWASH?

BECAUSE THEY HAVE BAT BREATH!

HOW DO YOU GET DRACULA'S AUTOGRAPH?

JOIN HIS FANG CLUB!

WHY DID SANTA GET A PARKING TICKET?

HE LEFT HIS SLEIGH IN A SNOW PARKING ZONE!

WHAT DOES MRS. CLAUS SAY WHEN SHE SEES BLACK CLOUDS?

"LOOKS LIKE RAIN, DEAR!"

WHAT DOES JACK FROST LIKE BEST AT SCHOOL?

SNOW AND TELL!

WHAT DOES SANTA WRITE ON FUNNY TEXT MESSAGES?

HHHOL!

WHAT DID THE SKELETON WRITE IN HER VALENTINE CARD?

"I LOVE EVERY BONE IN YOUR BODY!"

WHAT DID THE MAGNET SAY TO HER BOYFRIEND?

"YOU'RE VERY ATTRACTIVE!"

WHAT DID THE STAG SAY TO HIS GIRLFRIEND?

"I LOVE YOU DEERLY!"

WHAT DID THE GYMNAST SAY TO HER VALENTINE?

"I'M HEAD OVER HEELS IN LOVE WITH YOU!"

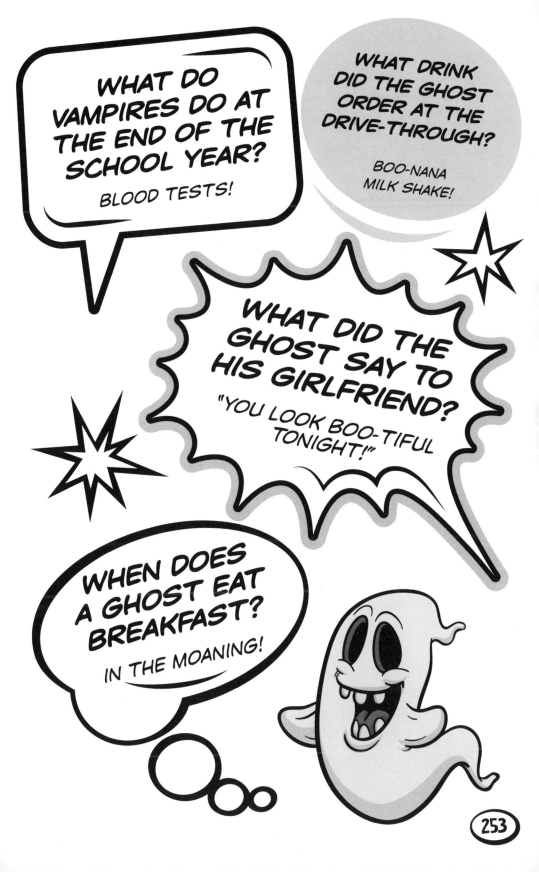

WHY IS IT SO COLD AT CHRISTMAS?

BECAUSE IT'S DECEMBRRRR!

WHAT DO YOU CALL SOMEONE WHO STEALS GIFT WRAP FROM THE RICH AND GIVES IT TO THE POOR?

RIBBON HOOD!

WHAT DID MRS. CLAUS SAY WHEN SANTA SHED A TEAR?

"DON'T GET SO SANTA-MENTAL, DARLING!"

WHAT KIND OF BALL DOESN'T BOUNCE?

A SNOWBALL!

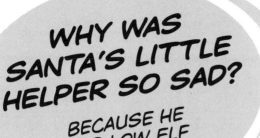

WHY WAS SANTA'S LITTLE HELPER SO SAD?

BECAUSE HE HAD LOW ELF ESTEEM!

WHAT DID THE CANDLE SAY TO THE OTHER CANDLE?

"I'M GOING OUT TONIGHT!"

WHAT DID THE CHRISTMAS TREE SAY TO THE DECORATIONS?

"AREN'T YOU TIRED OF JUST HANGING AROUND?"

WHAT DO SNOWMEN LIKE TO DO AFTER CHRISTMAS?

CHILL OUT!